TRANSFORMING
LEADERSHIP

Discover

Girl Scouts®

Connect

Take Action

TRANSFORMING
LEADERSHIP

Focusing on Outcomes of the
New Girl Scout Leadership Experience

GIRL SCOUTS OF THE USA

Chair, National Board of Directors
Patricia Diaz Dennis

Chief Executive Officer
Kathy Cloninger

Inquiries related to *Tranforming Leadership* should be directed to the Girl Scout Research Institute, Girl Scouts of the USA, 420 Fifth Avenue, New York, NY 10018-2798.

ISBN 978-0-88441-708-8

www.girlscouts.org

First Impression 2008
10 9 8 7 6 5 4 3

Contents

In Girl Scouts, leadership isn't just about building future leaders—it's about **building girl leaders for today.**

—Kathy Cloninger, CEO, Girl Scouts of the USA

THE NEW GIRL SCOUT LEADERSHIP EXPERIENCE

From founding libraries in America's heartland to establishing free medical clinics in India, each year 2.6 million Girl Scouts take the lead in bettering their communities and the world. Girl leaders have been at the heart of Girl Scouts since its founding in 1912, when Juliette Gordon Low recognized that developing girls' leadership abilities was critical for ensuring they would be the change-makers of the future.

Since Low's time, the world has changed dramatically. Social, cultural, and economic shifts that once took shape over a generation or more are now rapid and often have a global impact. This ever more complex and uncertain world clearly requires a new kind of leader—one who values diversity, inclusion, and collaboration and is committed to improving neighborhoods, communities, and the world.

Girl Scouts is, as it always has been, the organization best positioned to offer girls the tools they need to be successful leaders now and throughout their lives. As Girl Scouting approaches its 100th anniversary, the Movement is using its expertise to create a completely new approach for *what* girls do in Girl Scouting, *how* they do it, and how they will *benefit*.

A good leader is someone who works with others to **make things happen.**

—Annie, 17, Girl Scout Senior, North Carolina

Called the New Girl Scout Leadership Experience, this model engages girls in **discovering** themselves, **connecting** with others, and **taking action** to make the world a better place. This model begins with a definition of leadership that girls understand and believe in: a leader, girls say, is defined not only by the qualities and skills one has, but also by how those qualities and skills are used to make a difference in the world.

Research suggests that the youth development field is moving from the model of one individual leader to a model of shared leadership. This more inclusive and empowering approach is also the one girls most value (see *Exploring Girls' Leadership*, Girl Scout Research Institute, 2007). It encourages girls to take increasing responsibility for designing and implementing activities, and this results in extensive opportunities for them to see how their actions can impact the lives of others.

To develop and evaluate this model objectively, youth development experts, volunteers, and council and national staff identified 15 anticipated outcomes, or benefits, of the leadership experience. Tying the new program experience to outcomes serves three vital functions: to measure the impact of the experience; to determine what modifications are needed; and to communicate, to internal and external audiences, how girls are benefiting.

Leadership is knowing what you believe and putting it into action.

—Meaghan, 14, Girl Scout Cadette, Ohio

The Framework

The New Girl Scout Leadership Experience identifies three "keys" to leadership:

Discover: Girls understand themselves and their values and use their knowledge and skills to explore the world.

Connect: Girls care about, inspire, and team with others locally and globally.

Take Action: Girls act to make the world a better place.

All experiences in Girl Scouting incorporate the Discover, Connect, and Take Action keys to leadership. Girl Scout experiences are also, as much as possible, girl led and encourage learning by doing (experiential learning), and cooperative learning. These three processes promote the fun and friendship that have always been so integral to Girl Scouting.

As girls take part in Girl Scouts, facilitators can review the outcomes, and the signs of those outcomes, to gauge the benefits of the experience. The signs of the outcomes reflect what girls might think, say, or do—during and after a leadership experience—and help adults determine the success of the experience.

Outcomes charts, organized by the three Leadership Keys and by grade level, detail all 15 outcomes. Although detailed and comprehensive, the charts are an easy-to-use reference and can be used in varying ways. For example, volunteers coaching girls through experiences will want to know where related outcomes and signs are in the charts and how they fit into the leadership model. The signs are simply examples; they are not official assessments of ability and are not to be used to compare one girl to another.

Understanding the Model

The diagram at right shows the various components of the leadership experience and their tie to the larger goal that girls have the courage, confidence, and character to make the world a better place. When Discover, Connect, and Take Action activities are *girl led* and involve *learning by doing* and *cooperative learning*, girls achieve the desired and expected short-term leadership outcomes, ultimately resulting in Girl Scouting achieving its mission.

FOCUS OF
GIRL SCOUT
ACTIVITIES

**Discover
Connect
Take Action**

GIRL SCOUT
PROCESSES

**Girl Led
Learning by Doing
Cooperative Learning**

15 SHORT-TERM
AND INTERMEDIATE
OUTCOMES

**Girls gain specific
knowledge, skills,
attitudes, behaviors,
and values in
Girl Scouting.**

LONG-TERM OUTCOME

**Girls lead with
courage, confidence,
and character
to make the world
a better place.**

Outcomes in the New Girl Scout Leadership Experience

The diagram at right lists the 15 leadership outcomes and where they "live" within the Discover, Connect, and Take Action keys of leadership.

You may be wondering: How do you know that girls are having an effective leadership experience? Surely, discovering, connecting, and taking action are different for Girl Scout Brownies and Girl Scout Seniors.

The signs are what let adults know if girls at each grade level are achieving leadership skills. Checking the outcomes is like noting road signs on a journey—the signs that let you know you're getting closer to your destination. Similarly, seeing the age-appropriate signs during Girl Scout activities lets adults know that girls are achieving the intended outcomes.

Definitions of each outcome, and the signs for each, are organized in user-friendly reference tables beginning on page 23. Each outcome has its own reference table, as does each grade level. The tables are organized exactly as they are listed in the diagram at right, under the Discover, Connect, and Take Action keys to leadership.

Discover

+

Connect

+

Take Action

=

Leadership

1 Girls develop a strong sense of self.

2 Girls develop positive values.

3 Girls gain practical life skills.

4 Girls seek challenges in the world.

5 Girls develop critical thinking.

1 Girls develop healthy relationships.

2 Girls promote cooperation
and team building.

3 Girls can resolve conflicts.

4 Girls advance diversity in
a multicultural world.

5 Girls feel connected to their
communities, locally and globally.

1 Girls can identify community needs.

2 Girls are resourceful problem solvers.

3 Girls advocate for themselves and
others, locally and globally.

4 Girls educate and inspire others to act.

5 Girls feel empowered to make
a difference in the world.

Reading the Outcome Reference Tables

Each outcome reference table has six sections, one for each of the six Girl Scout grade levels:

Girl Scout Daisy (grades K–1)
Girl Scout Brownie (grades 2–3)
Girl Scout Junior (grades 4–5)
Girl Scout Cadette (grades 6–8)
Girl Scout Senior (grades 9–10)
Girl Scout Ambassador (grades 11–12)

Most likely, you will zero in on those outcomes you find most meaningful—ones that relate to a specific grade level or a specific impact on girls.

The chart at right shows one section of an outcome reference table and what each row and column mean.

This heading shows where the outcome belongs within the three keys to leadership development (Discover, Connect, Take Action).

This part of the table names the outcome and gives its definition.

Connect

OUTCOME

1

Girls develop healthy relationships.
Girls learn to form and maintain meaningful and caring relationships, communicate effectively, protect their rights in relationships, and know when to seek help from others.

GIRL SCOUT GRADE LEVEL	BY GRADE LEVEL Girls...	SAMPLE INDICATORS/SIGNS When the outcome is achieved, girls might... *
Brownie 2–3	begin to understand how their behavior contributes to maintaining healthy relationships.	identify healthy/unhealthy behaviors (e.g., honesty, caring, bullying) when presented with a relationship scenario.
	are better able to show empathy toward others.	make empathetic statements (e.g., "I helped Kim with that because she was getting frustrated") and/or report being more caring in their interactions with others.

This column shows the Girl Scout grade level.

This column defines the outcome for each grade level.

This column gives the signs of what girls might do or say that shows they achieved the outcome.

Using the Outcome Reference Tables

The outcome reference tables are being used to create resources and awards to ensure that girls engage in activities that lead to leadership skills. The Girl Scout Research Institute is using the tables to design a national system of outcomes measurement. Councils can also use the tables in a variety of ways, even focusing on one particular outcome at a time. Keep in mind, however, that according to the Girl Scout approach, leadership is the result of discovering, connecting, and taking action, so it is important to incorporate outcomes from all three Leadership Keys.

When Implementing Girl Scout Program

The signs in the outcome reference tables can give council staff ideas about how to design activities. A council, for example, may want to organize activities that help Girl Scout Cadettes feel empowered to make a difference in the world. The Take Action outcome reference table suggests that this can be accomplished at the Cadette level by providing opportunities for girls to feel that their opinions, ideas, and contributions are taken seriously by adults.

When Writing a Grant Proposal

Suppose a council fund development team is writing a grant proposal to support a program that helps Girl Scout Juniors develop a strong sense of self. The Discover outcome reference tables can be used to explain to potential funders what a strong sense of self means for this grade level and what its signs are. The fund development team can then include this information in its grant proposal.

When Training Volunteers

Suppose a council adult learning team wants to guide volunteers on partnering with Girl Scout Juniors so that the girls advance diversity. The Connect outcome reference table shows that for Girl Scout Juniors, advancing diversity means being able to identify discrimination and being more aware of ways to promote inclusiveness. The indicators suggest that the adult learning team should select activities for volunteer development that focus on how Girl Scout Juniors might identify discrimination.

When Recruiting

Suppose a council membership team wants to recruit adult volunteers based on a community's specific needs. The council could, for example, choose the outcome of gaining practical life skills, with a focus on healthy living. Outcomes from across all grade levels could be used to appeal to a broad range of volunteers. The membership team can also look at the indicators in the reference table to detail the signs of this outcome—further incentive for healthy-minded adults to volunteer in the community.

SHARE HOW YOU USE THE TABLES

As you discover other ways to make use of the reference tables, e-mail the Girl Scout Research Institute (gsresearch@girlscouts.org) so your ideas can be shared with other councils and Girl Scouts of the USA.

What leadership means to me is bringing others together as one and helping them **do things they have never tried before.**

—Shelby, 11, Girl Scout Junior, Colorado

Looking Ahead

Now that we have begun to chart the benefits of the New Girl Scout Leadership Experience and orient staff and volunteers to those benefits, plans are under way to develop measurement systems.

Through spring 2008, the GSRI will test measurements of the New Girl Scout Leadership Experience outcomes and program processes in a pilot study. Developing the signs for how the processes of girl led, learning by doing, and cooperative learning look for each grade level will be a major part of the work. The results will provide a baseline for future comparisons and initial measurement tools that will be ready in time for the 2008 National Council Session. The GSRI is also working with councils to develop a five-year plan for an integrated local/national outcomes measurement system. *Exploring Girls' Leadership* and an original study (forthcoming 2008) will further illuminate what leadership means for girls, which factors encourage them to aspire to leadership, and how Girl Scouting can make a difference.

The New Girl Scout Leadership Experience represents a leap forward in how Girl Scouting builds girls of courage, confidence, and character. By achieving the intended outcomes, girls will be prepared to be leaders who make the world a better place.

OUTCOMES ARRANGED BY
LEADERSHIP KEY

Discover

Connect

Take Action

Discover

Girls understand themselves and their values and use their knowledge and skills to explore the world.

OUTCOMES

1 Girls develop a strong sense of self.

2 Girls develop positive values.

3 Girls gain practical life skills.

4 Girls seek challenges in the world.

5 Girls develop critical thinking.

Discover

OUTCOME	Girls develop a strong sense of self.
1	Girls have confidence in themselves and their abilities, feel they are able to achieve their goals, and form positive gender, social, and cultural identities.

GIRL SCOUT GRADE LEVEL	BY GRADE LEVEL Girls…	SAMPLE INDICATORS/SIGNS When the outcome is achieved, girls might… *
Daisy K–1	are better able to recognize their strengths and abilities.	make positive statements about their abilities or demonstrate to others what they can do (e.g., "I was a good friend to Luna today").
Brownie 2–3	positively identify with their gender and cultural, linguistic, racial, and ethnic groups.	name things they like about being a girl. recognize how their characteristics make them unique (e.g., when drawing a picture of themselves, a girl can say, "I am Korean, and I speak Korean and English").
	have increased confidence in their abilities.	express pride in their accomplishments when speaking with others.
Junior 4–5	are better able to recognize how situations, attitudes, and the behaviors of others affect their sense of self.	compare how various situations (home, school, etc.) bring out various aspects of self.
	gain a clearer sense of their individual identities in relation to, and apart from, outside influences.	report increased confidence in dealing with outside pressures that try to dictate their thoughts and behaviors (e.g., peer pressure, advertising, cultural traditions).
Cadette 6–8	are better able to negotiate the effects of sociocultural factors, gender issues, and stereotyping/bias on to their sense of self.	describe how cultural influences affect their self-image (e.g., magazines dictating "right" body shape and size; effects of racist/sexist comments). make use of strategies to resist peer pressure (e.g., communicate with confidence, take responsibility for own actions).
	show an increase in self-efficacy.	report increased belief in their ability to achieve personal goals.
Senior 9–10	are better able to recognize and address personal and social barriers to reaching personal goals.	make connections between societal issues (e.g., prejudice based on gender or race) and their opportunities to achieve goals. report on ways they overcame gender, ethnic, and/or economic challenges to achieving their goals.
	are better able to recognize the multiple demands and expectations of others while establishing their own individuality.	describe challenges they face in finding a balance between accepting group beliefs and thinking/making decisions for themselves.
Ambassador 11–12	feel they are better equipped to pursue future/life goals.	report that they have options and possibilities for pursuing life/career goals. report increased confidence to get the job/education they envision.
	increase their sense of autonomy.	report being more self-reliant.

*Can you think of other sample indicators/signs?

Discover

Girls develop positive values.

Girls form their beliefs and values based on the Girl Scout Promise and Law, learn to consider ethical aspects of situations, and are committed to social justice and community service and action.

GIRL SCOUT GRADE LEVEL	BY GRADE LEVEL Girls...	SAMPLE INDICATORS/SIGNS When the outcome is achieved, girls might... *
Daisy K–1	begin to understand the values inherent in the Girl Scout Promise and Law.	identify actions that are fair/unfair, honest/dishonest in various scenarios.
	recognize that their choices of actions or words have an effect on others and the environment.	give an example of when their actions made something better for someone else.
Brownie 2–3	begin to apply values inherent in the Girl Scout Promise and Law in various contexts.	explain how they will take responsibility on the playground, at home, and at school.
	are better able to examine positive and negative effects of people's actions on others and the environment.	explain the difference between right and wrong choices. provide alternative choices to actions that harm the environment (e.g., throw plastic bottles in recycle bin, not in trash can).
Junior 4–5	gain greater understanding of ethical decision-making in their lives.	give examples of using the Girl Scout Promise and Law in deciding to "do what's right."
	have increased commitment to engage in sustainable community service and action.	feel it's important to help people and the environment in ways that will have a long-term positive impact. exhibit increased interest in Take Action Projects on issues of fairness and social justice in their communities.
Cadette 6–8	are better able to examine their own and others' values from individual, cultural, and global perspectives.	report greater appreciation for the diversity of values based on individual and/or cultural differences.
	demonstrate increased commitment to addressing issues of fairness, ethics, and justice in their communities.	identify instances that raise questions about issues of fairness, ethics, and/or social justice in their communities.
Senior 9–10	are better able to recognize and resolve ethical dilemmas.	give examples of making ethical decisions in their everyday lives and can explain why they made them (e.g., consider both direct and indirect consequences of their actions).
	strengthen their own and others' commitment to being socially, politically, and environmentally engaged citizens of their communities.	report increased positive attitudes of social responsibility and citizenship.
Ambassador 11–12	act consistently with a considered and self-determined set of values.	choose educational and career goals in line with the values they consider important.
	demonstrate commitment to promoting sustainable solutions to regional, national, and/or global problems.	report increased interest in learning more about making a sustainable impact beyond their local communities.

*Can you think of other sample indicators/signs?

Discover

Girls gain practical life skills—girls practice healthy living.**

Girls gain skills that prepare them for a positive, healthy, and independent future.

GIRL SCOUT GRADE LEVEL	BY GRADE LEVEL Girls...	SAMPLE INDICATORS/SIGNS When the outcome is achieved, girls might... *
Daisy K–1	gain greater knowledge of what is healthy for mind and body.	name behaviors that contribute to good health (e.g., eating fruit, getting exercise).
Brownie 2–3	are better at making healthy choices and minimizing unhealthy behaviors.	identify two hours of after-school sports as healthier than two hours of after-school computer games. name healthy choices they make (e.g., walking every day, choosing healthy snacks).
Junior 4–5	gain greater understanding of what it means to be emotionally and physically healthy.	describe how being stressed can affect physical health.
	are more aware of family, cultural, and media influences on making healthy choices.	list ways in which media promotes/inhibits healthy behavior (e.g., fast food ads).
Cadette 6–8	are increasingly committed to practicing and promoting healthy behavior.	report increased interest in learning more about how exercise, diet, relaxation, and other activities can give balance to their lives.
	are more knowledgeable about how family and cultural differences affect healthy living.	give examples of various cultures' definitions and practices of healthy living.
Senior 9–10	act as role models for younger girls in making healthy choices.	describe strategies for resisting pressure to engage in unhealthy behaviors (e.g., alcohol use or unhealthy dieting).
	show cultural sensitivity in their efforts to promote healthy living in their communities.	report increased knowledge of specific health needs in their diverse communities (e.g., responsive to religious or cultural beliefs).
Ambassador 11–12	are better able to address health issues in their lives, their local communities, and globally.	report using self-care practices to bring balance to their lives. identify ways their school's health education could better address the needs of young women.
	are more interested in leading and/or participating in advocacy projects related to health issues, globally or locally.	report increased knowledge of organizations that advocate for health-related issues, locally or globally.

*Can you think of other sample indicators/signs?

**Healthy Living is one example of a practical life skill. Outcomes and indicators for other practical skills will be developed over time.

Discover

Girls seek challenges in the world.
Girls develop positive attitudes toward learning, seek opportunities for expanding their knowledge and skills, set challenging goals for themselves, and take appropriate risks.

GIRL SCOUT GRADE LEVEL	BY GRADE LEVEL Girls...	SAMPLE INDICATORS/SIGNS When the outcome is achieved, girls might... *
Daisy K–1	demonstrate increased interest in learning new skills.	ask lots of questions/make lots of observations about the world around them.
Brownie 2–3	are more open to learning or doing new and challenging things.	enjoy trying new activities (e.g., building a fire, pitching a tent). report doing things they thought they couldn't do.
	recognize that one can learn from mistakes.	feel it is OK to make mistakes and might describe an instance in their own lives where they learned from a mistake.
Junior 4–5	increasingly recognize that positive risk-taking is important to personal growth and leadership.	when asked to identify attitudes important to accomplishing goals, mention risk-taking and give examples from their own lives.
	are better at exploring new skills and ideas.	report using a variety of resources to pursue topics of interest (e.g., the Internet, popular culture, art, poetry).
Cadette 6–8	are better able to distinguish positive and negative risk-taking.	when given risk-taking scenarios, identify and distinguish between positive and negative risk (e.g., riding with a driver who has been drinking vs. calling home for a ride even though parents will be angry).
	recognize the importance of challenging oneself for one's positive growth.	report how setting challenging goals helped them do better in school.
Senior 9–10	demonstrate increased enthusiasm for learning new skills and ideas and expanding existing ones.	increasingly offer their own ideas for exploring new topics or making existing ones more challenging.
	show increased courage to challenge their own and others' beliefs and opinions.	engage in a discussion with someone who has different political views. express preferences even when they differ from the majority's opinion.
Ambassador 11–12	increasingly set challenging goals for the future.	see themselves in roles/positions they previously considered unattainable.
	have increased confidence to discuss and address challenging issues and contradictions in their lives and in their local and global communities.	look for ways personal habits conflict with achieving goals that are important to them (e.g., fighting global warming). learn more about a controversial issue from someone who has experienced injustice or from a victim's advocate.

*Can you think of other sample indicators/signs?

Discover

Girls develop critical thinking.

Girls learn to examine ideas from a variety of viewpoints and further use critical thinking to explore implications of gender issues for their lives and their leadership development.

GIRL SCOUT GRADE LEVEL	BY GRADE LEVEL Girls...	SAMPLE INDICATORS/SIGNS When the outcome is achieved, girls might... *
Daisy K–1	recognize that the thoughts and feelings of others can vary from their own.	make statements that show they recognize another's feelings or opinions, such as "You are sad" and/or "You are happy."
Brownie 2–3	are increasingly able to consider other viewpoints in deciding what to do or believe.	listen to and consider each others' opinions when making decisions.
	are better able to recognize and examine stereotypes (based on gender, race, income, ability, etc.) that they encounter.	identify ways they or others are treated differently based on gender, race, income, and ability and can explain why stereotyping is harmful.
Junior 4–5	show greater skill in gathering and evaluating information.	consider various factors before deciding what to believe (e.g., how credible is the source of information, is there a hidden agenda).
	are better able to consider multiple perspectives on issues.	show increased interest in learning about different sides of issues (e.g., with other girls, in public forums).
Cadette 6–8	are better able to examine issues and ideas from various perspectives.	debate or discuss various perspectives on an issue they are concerned about (e.g., women's rights, global warming).
	have increased understanding of positive and negative ways that media impact their own and others' lives.	give examples of how TV shows can promote sexism, racism, and other -isms or how the Internet can promote freedom of information or allow disinformation.
Senior 9–10	are better able to analyze their own and others' thinking processess.	give examples of the steps they followed and why they made a specific decision or formed an opinion.
	are better able to apply critical thinking skills to challenge stereotypes and biases.	question assumptions behind inequities they encounter (e.g., female athletes earning less than male athletes).
Ambassador 11–12	are increasingly able to address local/global/societal barriers to women's leadership.	discuss various obstacles facing women leaders now and in the past (e.g., discrimination based on gender, race, class, ability). express interest in Take Action Projects that address gender inequality, locally or globally.

*Can you think of other sample indicators/signs?

Connect

Girls care about, inspire, and team with others locally and globally.

OUTCOMES

1 **Girls develop healthy relationships.**

2 **Girls promote cooperation and team building.**

3 **Girls can resolve conflicts.**

4 **Girls advance diversity in a multicultural world.**

5 **Girls feel connected to their communities, locally and globally.**

Girls develop healthy relationships.

Girls learn to form and maintain meaningful and caring relationships, communicate effectively, protect their rights in relationships, and know when to seek help from others.

GIRL SCOUT GRADE LEVEL	BY GRADE LEVEL Girls...	SAMPLE INDICATORS/SIGNS When the outcome is achieved, girls might... *
Daisy K–1	are better able to demonstrate helpful and caring behavior.	spontaneously offer to help someone in need of assistance (e.g., opening door, carrying package).
	are better able to identify and communicate their feelings to others.	express their feelings verbally (e.g., "I feel lonely when the others don't include me"), rather than nonverbally (e.g., crying, withdrawing, lashing out).
Brownie 2–3	begin to understand how their behavior contributes to maintaining healthy relationships.	identify healthy/unhealthy behaviors (e.g., honesty, caring, bullying) when presented with a relationship scenario.
	are better able to show empathy toward others.	make empathetic statements (e.g., "I helped Kim with that because she was getting frustrated") and/or report being more caring in their interactions with others.
Junior 4–5	strengthen communication skills for maintaining healthy relationships.	name communication strategies that help them in their relationships (e.g., listening to the ideas of others, encouraging others instead of criticizing them).
	are more competent in addressing negative treatment by others.	identify bullying tactics and aggressive behaviors in others. name people they can turn to for help when dealing with difficulties in relationships.
Cadette 6–8	have more positive, trusting relationships with others.	report having at least one girl or adult they can talk to about anything.
	are able to use positive communication and relationship-building skills.	give examples of behaviors they use to promote mutual respect, trust, and understanding.
	feel more comfortable with new feelings that accompany adolescence and ways of expressing feelings in relationships, including sexual feelings.	talk about healthy decision-making (e.g., encouraging self-respect in themselves and others) when presented with relationship scenarios.
Senior 9–10	are better able to recognize and address challenges to forming and maintaining healthy relationships with others.	recognize that people hold different beliefs about relationships (e.g., based on gender, culture). identify behaviors that hinder the development of positive relationships (e.g., backstabbing, gossip).
	have increased knowledge of what healthy dating entails.	report that it is important to be able to communicate their needs effectively. recognize unhealthy dating behaviors when presented with a dating scenario.
Ambassador 11–12	strengthen strategies for maintaining healthy relationships.	give examples of using assertive behaviors and might explain when and why these work/don't work.
	are better able to protect their rights in relationships.	actively seek information on healthy dating behaviors (e.g., how to avoid risky sexual activity, where to get help for abusive relationships). report knowing whom to contact when faced with unhealthy relationships (e.g., a hotline, school counselor, trusted adults).

*Can you think of other sample indicators/signs?

Connect

Girls promote cooperation and team building.

Girls recognize the value of working together and learn to make decisions that benefit the whole group. They can build effective teams, learn to be accountable for shared goals, and show recognition for others' accomplishments and contributions.

GIRL SCOUT GRADE LEVEL	BY GRADE LEVEL Girls...	SAMPLE INDICATORS/SIGNS When the outcome is achieved, girls might... *
Daisy K–1	begin to learn how to work well with others.	name something about themselves that helps them work well in a group (e.g., "I listen well").
Brownie 2–3	gain a better understanding of cooperative and team-building skills.	be able to identify strengths or talents that each girl brings to group projects (e.g., "Monica is good at drawing and I am a really good singer"). describe ways to make group projects more fun (e.g., switching roles, brainstorming, listening to each other).
Junior 4–5	are better able to initiate and maintain cooperation on their teams.	with minimal adult guidance, apply specific strategies for promoting cooperation (e.g., listening to all ideas, rotating tasks and roles, developing shared goals).
	increasingly recognize how cooperation contributes to a project's success.	consistently prefer solving problems in teams or as a group and explain why this can be more effective than working alone.
Cadette 6–8	have a greater understanding of team building.	list criteria for what makes a good team (e.g., clear roles, trust, respect, diversity).
	are better able to address obstacles to effective group work and team building.	describe obstacles to group work (e.g., not being willing to compromise, concern with individual interests over group goals, always wanting to be the person talking) and suggest possible solutions.
Senior 9–10	strengthen their abilities to build effective teams to accomplish shared goals.	identify specific strategies for building effective teams (e.g., paying attention to interests, strengths, team dynamics). demonstrate that they can reach consensus on common goals.
	are committed to mentoring others on effective strategies for cooperative work and team building.	help others work better as a team (e.g., encourage them to reach consensus on project goals, create "listening" exercises for other girls, recognize each others' achievements).
Ambassador 11–12	are able to promote cooperation and effective team building in their communities.	describe how their Take Action Project encouraged sustained cooperation among various people/organizations in their communities.
	recognize the value of cooperation and team building for effective leadership and for their future careers.	report that cooperation and team-building skills helped them in other spheres of their lives.

*Can you think of other sample indicators/signs?

Connect

Girls can resolve conflicts.

Girls learn to recognize and analyze different conflict situations and develop skills for constructive conflict resolution and prevention.

GIRL SCOUT GRADE LEVEL	BY GRADE LEVEL Girls...	SAMPLE INDICATORS/SIGNS When the outcome is achieved, girls might... *
Daisy K–1	begin to understand what conflict is.	give examples of conflict situations in their lives.
	learn simple conflict-resolution strategies.	express feelings using "I statements" when they find themselves in a conflict situation (e.g., "I'm sorry I hurt your feelings").
Brownie 2–3	are better able to apply basic strategies for conflict resolution when conflicts arise.	name helpful ways to deal with anger/frustration in a conflict (e.g., talk things out instead of acting out or hitting).
Junior 4–5	are better able to select conflict-resolution strategies to fit the situation.	describe and/or demonstrate conflict-resolution responses for various settings, such as home, school, or neighborhood. explain why one strategy works in one situation but not another (e.g., at home can resolve conflict with sibling by talking with parent; but this would not work at the playground).
	are better at analyzing conflict situations.	give reasons why they fight with each other.
Cadette 6–8	strengthen their conflict-resolution and prevention strategies.	say how they manage their emotions (e.g., anger, hurt) to diffuse a conflict situation (e.g., don't lose their temper).
	have a greater understanding of how conflict-resolution skills contribute to effective leadership.	give examples of how their conflict-resolution skills helped them succeed on a project.
Senior 9–10	can increasingly apply effective strategies for conflict resolution and prevention.	report using effective anger-management skills and strategies.
	are better able to analyze conflict situations in their communities and globally, and offer possible solutions.	identify deeper social roots of conflicts among various groups in their communities (e.g., conflicting interests, racism, sexism, other forms of prejudice). describe how certain conflicts in their communities can be avoided by applying prevention strategies they learned.
Ambassador 11–12	are better able to develop their own approaches to conflict resolution and prevention.	give examples of how they adapted conflict-resolution strategies to personal situations (e.g., argument with parent or at a teen dance).
	increasingly apply conflict-resolution skills to working toward peaceful and fair relations in their communities.	report using conflict-resolution skills to contribute to peace and fairness in their communities (e.g., become peer mediators at school).

*Can you think of other sample indicators/signs?

Connect

Girls advance diversity in a multicultural world.

Girls learn to think and act in a way that promotes an inclusive environment, respecting and valuing diverse backgrounds, viewpoints, and life experiences.

GIRL SCOUT GRADE LEVEL	BY GRADE LEVEL Girls...	SAMPLE INDICATORS/SIGNS When the outcome is achieved, girls might... *
Daisy K–1	recognize that it's OK to be different.	identify characteristics that make them different from other girls (e.g., hair color, food preferences, other likes/dislikes, family structure).
	increasingly relate to others in an inclusive manner.	notice when others are excluded from activities (e.g., "It's not fair that no one is playing with Annie").
Brownie 2–3	begin to understand the meaning of diversity.	explore their differences and similarities (e.g., based on culture, ethnicity, ability, life experiences).
	strengthen their appreciation of differences in others.	not make fun—and might encourage others not to make fun—of those who look/talk/behave differently from themselves.
Junior 4–5	recognize the value of promoting diversity in the world.	report that it's important to promote inclusiveness in various contexts and can explain why. demonstrate increased interest in interacting with others from different backgrounds (e.g., ethnicity, culture, class, religion, gender, ability).
	develop greater awareness of various forms of discrimination in the world.	when presented with various situations (e.g., from stories, news, movies, music, or their community), identify discrimination.
Cadette 6–8	are more aware of the issues, perspectives, and experiences of people from various backgrounds, locally and globally.	identify main challenges as well as privileges that various groups experience in today's world (e.g., women and men, ethnicities, abilities).
	learn strategies for promoting diversity and creating more inclusive environments.	actively include people of diverse backgrounds in their activities/events. actively encourage others to behave in inclusive ways (e.g., petition for a wheelchair-accessible park gazebo, use effective ways to speak out against exclusion and discrimination).
	can examine the negative impact of stereotyping, prejudice, discrimination, and privilege on their lives and the lives of others.	when given examples from the media, describe the negative impact of stereotyping and prejudice (based on ethnicity, religion, language, class, sexuality, gender, and ability).
Senior 9–10	are actively engaged in promoting diversity and tolerance.	create materials to educate others on how to contribute to more inclusive environments with their peers, in school, in their neighborhoods, etc. (e.g., Web sites, how-to guides, events).
	are increasingly able to address challenges to promoting inclusive attitudes and diversity.	plan activities/events showing the harmful consequences of prejudice and discrimination on people in their communities. place high value on empathy and open-mindedness when interacting with people from diverse backgrounds.
Ambassador 11–12	are actively engaged in promoting diversity and tolerance, locally and/or globally.	give examples of meaningful collaboration with people from diverse backgrounds for their global Take Action Projects.
	are increasingly able to address various challenges to promoting inclusive attitudes and diversity, locally and/or globally.	identify the main reasons that prevent people from embracing diversity (e.g., racism, sexism, lack of education, lack of empathy) and can suggest possible solutions (e.g., increase understanding by educating people about diverse cultural values and traditions).

*Can you think of other sample indicators/signs?

Connect

Girls feel connected to their communities, locally and globally.

Girls feel that they are part of a larger community and recognize the importance of building diverse, supportive, social networks for their personal and leadership development.

GIRL SCOUT GRADE LEVEL	BY GRADE LEVEL Girls...	SAMPLE INDICATORS/SIGNS When the outcome is achieved, girls might... *
Daisy K–1	are better able to identify people and places that make up their community and understand their various contributions.	identify people who provide services in their communities (e.g., doctors provide medical care, teachers provide education).
	gain increased understanding of how they belong to various groups in their communities.	give examples of the various groups to which they belong (e.g., Girl Scouts, sports team, religious community).
Brownie 2–3	have greater interest in participating in community events, activities, and social networks.	positively describe their participation in at least one community event and/or activity (e.g., help at a cancer walk, start a "Park Keeper" club).
	recognize the importance of being part of a larger community.	give examples of how group/community members help and support each other (e.g., in their neighborhood, school).
Junior 4–5	are better able to recognize the importance of knowing about, and actively participating in, community groups.	identify various sources of information for what is going on in their communities (e.g., the Internet, magazines, interviews with people). describe how being involved in their communities resulted in stronger connections to others (e.g., Take Action Project resulted in an adult from the community volunteering to teach girls a particular skill).
	begin to feel part of a larger community of girls/women.	enjoy connecting with girls/women locally, nationally, or globally (e.g., through reading about them, face-to-face interactions, e-mail).
Cadette 6–8	strengthen existing relationships and seek to create new connections with others in their communities.	use various ways to connect with others, locally and globally (e.g., the Internet, get-togethers, *destinations*, events). feel more confident contacting community members for help with community service and action projects (e.g., teachers, youth organizations, after-school clubs).
	gain greater understanding of the importance of community networks for themselves and others.	describe how their participation in larger communities supported their personal and leadership goals (e.g., provided safe environment, helped gain skills).
Senior 9–10	actively seek to bring people together in local and global networks.	give an example of organizing a local or global event that brought together diverse members of their communities. develop friendships with Girl Guides from other countries (e.g., e-mail pals, joint international projects, visits to World Centers).
	feel that their connections with diverse members of their communities are important resources for personal and leadership development.	make friends with girls/women through the World Association of Girl Guides and Girl Scouts (WAGGGS) and can explain why these connections are important to them.
Ambassador 11–12	have extensive feelings of connection with their local and global communities.	report more positive attitudes toward different members of their communities. place high value on providing support for diverse members of their communities.

*Can you think of other sample indicators/signs?

Take Action

Girls act to make the
world a better place.

OUTCOMES

1 **Girls can identify community needs.**

2 **Girls are resourceful problem solvers.**

3 **Girls advocate for themselves and others, locally and globally.**

4 **Girls educate and inspire others to act.**

5 **Girls feel empowered to make a difference in the world.**

Take Action

OUTCOME 1 | Girls can identify community needs.

Girls learn to identify issues in their local and global communities and come up with realistic possibilities for action.

GIRL SCOUT GRADE LEVEL	BY GRADE LEVEL Girls...	SAMPLE INDICATORS/SIGNS When the outcome is achieved, girls might... *
Daisy K–1	gain increased knowledge of their communities' assets.	name people/places they consider helpful and valuable in their communities.
Brownie 2–3	develop basic strategies to identify community issues.	use various ways to gain information about their communities (e.g., the Internet, library, personal interviews). list things about their community that are valuable and things that could be improved.
Brownie 2–3	gain a greater understanding of how Take Action Projects might impact their communities.	explain how the issue they agreed to take action on can benefit their community (e.g., other girls, families, a church).
Junior 4–5	learn to use strategies to determine issues that deserve action.	use community asset mapping to identify opportunities to better their communities.
Junior 4–5	are better able to determine whether projects can be realistically accomplished.	consider time and/or financial constraints before selecting an issue to tackle.
Cadette 6–8	strengthen their ability to decide which community issue deserves action.	report using a variety of tools (e.g., community mapping, interviewing, observations) to identify needs, assets, and potential impact of their planned projects.
Cadette 6–8	begin to address deeper causes of issues in their communities.	identify multiple causes for a problem they wish to address. explain the difference between a quick fix and long-term solutions (e.g., reading to someone learning English as a second language vs. teaching someone to read).
Senior 9–10	are more skilled in identifying their local or global communities' needs that they can realistically address.	report considering multiple factors before deciding on the appropriateness of a project for their community (e.g., feasibility, balance of assets and needs, sustainable impact). seek advice from community members/leaders before selecting issues for action.
Senior 9–10	choose Take Action Projects that aim to address deeper causes of issues in their communities.	feel confident using tools that help them identify root causes of community problems (e.g., causal mapping).
Ambassador 11–12	are more skilled in identifying issues that balance feasibility with achieving long-term changes in their local or global communities.	identify community partners that can continue their project goals into the future.
Ambassador 11–12	choose Take Action Projects that aim to address deeper causes of issues in their communities.	interview staff and residents of a homeless shelter to identify root causes of homelessness in that community.

*Can you think of other sample indicators/signs?

Take Action

Girls are resourceful problem solvers.
Girls can use their knowledge and skills to set up and implement creative and effective "action plans," locate tools and resources they need, and know when, where, and how to enlist help from others.

GIRL SCOUT GRADE LEVEL	BY GRADE LEVEL Girls...	SAMPLE INDICATORS/SIGNS When the outcome is achieved, girls might... *
Daisy K–1	learn the basics of planning a project.	with adult guidance, make a list of resources needed to complete their project (e.g., materials for creating get-well cards for a children's hospital).
Brownie 2–3	are better able to develop a basic plan to reach a goal or a solution to a problem.	identify two or three steps and resources (people, materials, information) needed to reach a goal or solve a problem (e.g., how to get ready for camp).
	are better able to create alternative solutions to problems.	reflect on a real-life problem or a scenario and state an alternative solution, such as "Next time, I will do this instead."
Junior 4–5	are better able to create an "action plan" for their projects.	outline steps, resources, and time lines and assign responsibilities for their project with minimal adult guidance. report increased confidence in creating action plans for their goals.
	gain a greater ability to locate and use resources that will help accomplish their project goals.	feel confident contacting community partners who can help them achieve their goals (e.g., school officials who can display girls' fliers on bulletin boards).
Cadette 6–8	are able to create and implement detailed action plans for their projects.	demonstrate independence in thinking through the required components of their action plans (e.g., location of resources, time lines, responsibilities). report being more able to keep themselves "on track," requesting adult help if needed.
	increasingly seek out community support and resources to help achieve their goals.	identify people/organizations in their communities to help on some aspect of their project (e.g., obtain editing guidance for media projects).
Senior 9–10	are better able to effectively plan and carry out action projects with minimal adult guidance.	create detailed action plans, organize, and coordinate with others in the community, managing time and anticipating possible problems and resource needs on their own.
	are able to assess their progress and adjust strategies as necessary.	identify alternative ways to accomplish goals if initial plans prove unsuccessful. identify things they could do better and/or differently next time they work on a community service or action project.
Ambassador 11–12	are better able to independently plan, organize, and manage Take Action Projects.	report increased knowledge and skill in various aspects of project planning and implementation. monitor their own progress and determine criteria for success.
	actively seek partnerships to achieve greater community participation and impact for their Take Action Projects.	describe their efforts to engage community partners—locally or globally—in the implementation of community service and action projects. explain how partnerships with others maximize the impact of their Take Action Projects.

*Can you think of other sample indicators/signs?

Take Action

Girls advocate for themselves and others, locally and globally.
Girls develop the ability to speak out on their own behalf and seek opportunities to act and speak on behalf of others.

GIRL SCOUT GRADE LEVEL	BY GRADE LEVEL Girls...	SAMPLE INDICATORS/SIGNS When the outcome is achieved, girls might... *
Daisy K–1	recognize that they can act on behalf of others.	recognize situations when they can "make something better" for someone else (e.g., through words or actions).
Brownie 2–3	gain a better understanding of their rights and those of others.	name rights people have in their schools, families, or communities (e.g., to be safe, to be treated fairly, to be heard).
	learn and begin to apply basic advocacy skills.	define what advocacy means and give examples of advocates in their communities. use words or actions to show concern and intervene when another person is not being treated well (e.g., stand up for someone being teased).
Junior 4–5	strengthen their abilities to effectively speak out or act for themselves and others.	identify concrete steps they can take to effect desired changes (e.g., who to contact about creating safer streets for bicycling in their neighborhood).
Cadette 6–8	recognize the importance of advocacy in accomplishing positive changes for themselves and others.	can give examples of how youth can influence and/or participate in community decision-making (e.g., influence the library to remain open longer, start a teen hotline, form an antidiscrimination group).
	gain greater ability to use specific advocacy skills to address issues of interest.	report using various strategies to speak out for themselves and others on issues of interest (e.g., writing letters, petitions, creating public announcements).
Senior 9–10	have a greater understanding of how the decisions and policies of various institutions have effects on their lives and the lives of others.	report increased knowledge about how public decisions in their schools, communities, and local governments affect people's private lives (e.g., decisions about education, juvenile justice).
	use advocacy skills and knowledge to be more active on behalf of a cause, issue, or person, locally or globally.	give examples of advocating for an issue in their school or neighborhood (e.g., more healthful cafeteria food, increased awareness of eating disorders, reproductive health, effects of poverty).
Ambassador 11–12	recognize that they have the rights and abilities to participate in the development of public policy that affects their lives and the lives of others.	report increased interest and confidence in participating in projects or initiatives that promote positive social changes.
	are better able to consider the community/global impact of their advocacy efforts.	describe how their advocacy efforts helped their community or the broader society.
	actively seek partnerships with other organizations that provide support and resources for their advocacy efforts.	report working with organizations that share their advocacy goals.

*Can you think of other sample indicators/signs?

Take Action

Girls learn to effectively explain their ideas to others and motivate them to get involved in community service and action.

GIRL SCOUT GRADE LEVEL	BY GRADE LEVEL Girls...	SAMPLE INDICATORS/SIGNS When the outcome is achieved, girls might... *
Daisy K–1	are better able to assist peers and seek help from them.	respond to requests for help/assistance with actions or words.
Brownie 2–3	are better able to explain their ideas or teach new skills to others.	demonstrate or teach a skill to other girls (e.g., how to sell cookies, how to make a puppet).
	can communicate their reasons for engaging in community service and action.	explain why they chose a community action project (e.g., meals to seniors, holiday gifts to needy children), how/why it benefited others, and what they learned from it.
Junior 4–5	learn various strategies to communicate and share Take Action Projects with others.	use various ways to tell others about their Take Action Projects (e.g., fliers, presentations). explain what makes a successful persuasive message/action for various audiences (e.g., presentation to peers, petitions to officials).
Cadette 6–8	show increased commitment to educate others on how to better their communities.	organize a show-and-tell for younger Girl Scouts to educate them about how to be more active in community affairs.
	are better able to identify and select various methods for informing others about their Take Action Projects.	report knowing how to tailor their messages to various audiences (e.g., young girls vs. senior citizens).
Senior 9–10	are better at inspiring and mobilizing others to become more engaged in community service and action.	shape messages (e.g., in a flier, speech, publication, or Web campaign) to explain the importance of taking action on an issue they care about. organize an awareness day in their schools on an issue they care about (e.g., emotional health, Internet safety).
Ambassador 11–12	are better able to evaluate the effectiveness of their efforts to reach/educate diverse audiences and can adjust their communication strategies accordingly.	implement innovative ways to access hard-to-reach audiences (e.g., using the Internet to engage remote rural populations). work with other youth/community organizations to spread their messages more effectively.

*Can you think of other sample indicators/signs?

Take Action

Girls feel empowered to make a difference in the world.

Girls feel empowered to use their leadership skills to effect change in their lives and their world and feel their contributions are valued in the larger community.

GIRL SCOUT GRADE LEVEL	BY GRADE LEVEL Girls...	SAMPLE INDICATORS/SIGNS When the outcome is achieved, girls might... *
Daisy K–1	feel their actions and words are important to others.	give an example of something they have done to make them feel like an important part of their group (e.g., help choose an activity, lead a game, help make up a rule).
Brownie 2–3	increasingly feel they have important roles and responsibilities in their groups and/or communities.	describe ways their actions contributed to bettering something (for their families, neighborhood, environment).
	exhibit increased determination to create changes for themselves and others.	give examples when they succeeded in making a positive change for themselves or others.
Junior 4–5	are more confident in their power to effect positive change.	describe various expressions of power around them (e.g., power over others, power to do something, power with others). explain how shared power helped them create better or longer-lasting changes (e.g., working together vs. doing it alone).
	feel they have greater opportunities for involvement in the decision-making of their communities.	give examples of when they participated in the decision-making processes in their Girl Scout council, church, school, etc.
Cadette 6–8	feel more valued by others for their ability to apply leaderships skills toward positive change.	feel that their opinions, ideas, and contributions are taken seriously by adults. express pride that their Take Action Projects improved functioning of some aspect of their communities (e.g., contributed to cleaner air, safer streets, better opportunities for young people).
	have increased confidence to participate in decision-making processes in their groups or communities.	show interest in providing and/or receiving input from community members on community issues.
Senior 9–10	are better able to address challenges to their feeling of empowerment.	identify internal and/or external barriers to feeling empowered to create change (e.g., not being taken seriously because they are "just kids"). describe strategies for ensuring that their voices and opinions are heard.
	feel they have greater access to community resources and more equal relationships with adults in their communities.	report that adults in their communities invite their input and/or participation in community affairs.
Ambassador 11–12	feel capable of using their skills to better the functioning and governance of communities, locally or globally.	create an action plan that could be implemented to include more young people in setting town priorities.
	feel their projects and ideas are valued/respected by stakeholders in their local and/or global communities.	give examples of positive reports (e.g., local news coverage) about their Take Action Projects.

*Can you think of other sample indicators/signs?

OUTCOMES ARRANGED BY
GRADE LEVEL

Daisy

Brownie

Junior

Cadette

Senior

Ambassador

Daisy

grades K–1

Girl Scout Daisies understand themselves and their values and use their knowledge and skills to explore the world.

DISCOVER OUTCOMES	BY GRADE LEVEL Girls...	SAMPLE INDICATORS/SIGNS When the outcome is achieved, girls might... *
Girls develop a strong sense of self: Girls have confidence in themselves and their abilities, feel they are able to achieve their goals, and form positive gender, social, and cultural identities.	are better able to recognize their strengths and abilities.	make positive statements about their abilities or demonstrate to others what they can do (e.g., "I was a good friend to Luna today").
Girls develop positive values: Girls form their beliefs and values based on the Girl Scout Promise and Law, learn to consider ethical aspects of situations, and are committed to social justice and community service and action.	begin to understand the values inherent in the Girl Scout Promise and Law.	identify actions that are fair/unfair, honest/dishonest in various scenarios.
	recognize that their choices of actions or words have an effect on others and the environment.	give an example of when their actions made something better for someone else.
Girls gain practical life skills—girls practice healthy living:** Girls gain skills that prepare them for a positive, healthy, and independent future.	gain greater knowledge of what is healthy for mind and body.	name behaviors that contribute to good health (e.g., eating fruit, getting exercise).
Girls seek challenges in the world: Girls develop positive attitudes toward learning, seek opportunities for expanding their knowledge and skills, set challenging goals for themselves, and take appropriate risks.	demonstrate increased interest in learning new skills.	ask lots of questions/make lots of observations about the world around them.
Girls develop critical thinking: Girls learn to examine ideas from a variety of viewpoints and further use critical thinking to explore implications of gender issues for their lives and their leadership development.	recognize that the thoughts and feelings of others can vary from their own.	make statements that show they recognize another's feelings or opinions, such as "You are sad" and/or "You are happy."

*Can you think of other sample indicators/signs?

**Healthy Living is one example of a practical life skill. Outcomes and indicators for other practical skills will be developed over time.

Girl Scout Daisies care about, inspire, and team with others locally and globally.

CONNECT OUTCOMES	BY GRADE LEVEL Girls...	SAMPLE INDICATORS/SIGNS When the outcome is achieved, girls might... *
Girls develop healthy relationships: Girls learn to form and maintain meaningful and caring relationships, communicate effectively, protect their rights in relationships, and know when to seek help from others.	are better able to demonstrate helpful and caring behavior.	spontaneously offer to help someone in need of assistance (e.g., opening door, carrying package).
	are better able to identify and communicate their feelings to others.	express their feelings verbally (e.g., "I feel lonely when the others don't include me"), rather than nonverbally (e.g., crying, withdrawing, lashing out).
Girls promote cooperation and team building: Girls recognize the value of working together and learn to make decisions that benefit the whole group. They can build effective teams, learn to be accountable for their shared goals, and show recognition for others' accomplishments and contributions.	begin to learn how to work well with others.	name something about themselves that helps them work well in a group (e.g., "I listen well").
Girls can resolve conflicts: Girls learn to recognize and analyze different conflict situations and develop skills for constructive conflict resolution and prevention.	begin to understand what conflict is.	give examples of conflict situations in their lives.
	learn simple conflict-resolution strategies.	express feelings using "I statements" when they find themselves in a conflict situation (e.g., "I'm sorry I hurt your feelings").
Girls advance diversity in a multicultural world: Girls learn to think and act in a way that promotes an inclusive environment, respecting and valuing diverse backgrounds, viewpoints, and life experiences.	recognize that it's OK to be different.	identify characteristics that make them different from other girls (e.g., hair color, food preferences, other likes/dislikes, family structure).
	increasingly relate to others in an inclusive manner.	notice when others are excluded from activities (e.g., "It's not fair that no one is playing with Annie").
Girls feel connected to their communities, locally and globally: Girls feel that they are part of a larger community and recognize the importance of building diverse, supportive social networks for their personal and leadership development.	are better able to identify people and places that make up their community and understand their various contributions.	identify people who provide services in their communities (e.g., doctors provide medical care, teachers provide education).
	gain increased understanding of how they belong to various groups in their communities.	give examples of the various groups to which they belong (e.g., Girl Scouts, sports team, religious community).

*Can you think of other sample indicators/signs?

Girl Scout Daisies act to make the world a better place.

TAKE ACTION OUTCOMES	BY GRADE LEVEL Girls...	SAMPLE INDICATORS/SIGNS When the outcome is achieved, girls might... *
Girls can identify community needs: Girls learn to identify issues in their local and global communities and come up with realistic possibilities for action.	gain increased knowledge of their communities' assets.	name people/places they consider helpful and valuable in their communities.
Girls are resourceful problem solvers: Girls can use their knowledge and skills to set up and implement creative and effective "action plans," locate tools and resources they need, and know when, where, and how to enlist help from others.	learn the basics of planning a project.	with adult guidance, make a list of resources needed to complete their project (e.g., materials for creating get-well cards for a children's hospital).
Girls advocate for themselves and others, locally and globally: Girls develop the ability to speak out on their own behalf and seek opportunities to act and speak on behalf of others.	recognize that they can act on behalf of others.	recognize situations when they can "make something better" for someone else (e.g., through words or actions).
Girls educate and inspire others to act: Girls learn to effectively explain their ideas to others and motivate them to get involved in community service and action.	are better able to assist peers and seek help from them.	respond to requests for help/assistance with actions or words.
Girls feel empowered to make a difference in the world: Girls feel empowered to use their leadership skills to effect change in their lives and their world, and feel their contributions are valued in the larger community.	feel their actions and words are important to others.	give an example of something they have done to make them feel like an important part of their group (e.g., help choose an activity, lead a game, help make up a rule).

*Can you think of other sample indicators/signs?

47

Brownie

grades 2–3

Girl Scout Brownies understand themselves and their values and use their knowledge and skills to explore the world.

DISCOVER OUTCOMES	BY GRADE LEVEL Girls...	SAMPLE INDICATORS/SIGNS When the outcome is achieved, girls might... *
Girls develop a strong sense of self: Girls have confidence in themselves and their abilities, feel they are able to achieve their goals, and form positive gender, social, and cultural identities.	positively identify with their gender and cultural, linguistic, racial, and ethnic groups.	name things they like about being a girl. recognize how their characteristics make them unique (e.g., when drawing a picture of themselves, a girl can say, "I am Korean, and I speak Korean and English").
	have increased confidence in their abilities.	express pride in their accomplishments when speaking with others.
Girls develop positive values: Girls form their beliefs and values based on the Girl Scout Promise and Law, learn to consider ethical aspects of situations, and are committed to social justice and community service and action.	begin to apply values inherent in the Girl Scout Promise and Law in various contexts.	explain how they will take responsibility on the playground, at home, and at school.
	are better able to examine positive and negative effects of people's actions on others and the environment.	explain the difference between right and wrong choices. provide alternative choices to actions that harm the environment (e.g., throw plastic bottles in recycle bin, not in trash can).
Girls gain practical life skills—girls practice healthy living:** Girls gain skills that prepare them for a positive, healthy, and independent future.	are better at making healthy choices and minimizing unhealthy behaviors.	identify two hours of after-school sports as healthier than two hours of after-school computer games. name healthy choices they make (e.g., walking every day, choosing healthful snacks).
Girls seek challenges in the world: Girls develop positive attitudes toward learning, seek opportunities for expanding their knowledge and skills, set challenging goals for themselves, and take appropriate risks.	are more open to learning or doing new and challenging things.	enjoy trying new activities (e.g., building a fire, pitching a tent). report doing things they thought they couldn't do.
	recognize that one can learn from mistakes.	feel it is OK to make mistakes and might describe an instance in their own lives where they learned from a mistake.
Girls develop critical thinking: Girls learn to examine ideas from a variety of viewpoints and further use critical thinking to explore implications of gender issues for their lives and their leadership development.	are increasingly able to consider other viewpoints in deciding what to do or believe.	listen to and consider each others' opinions when making decisions.
	are better able to recognize and examine stereotypes (based on gender, race, income, ability, etc.) that they encounter.	identify ways they or others are treated differently based on gender, race, income, and ability and can explain why stereotyping is harmful.

*Can you think of other sample indicators/signs?

**Healthy Living is one example of a practical life skill. Outcomes and indicators for other practical skills will be developed over time.

Girl Scout Brownies care about, inspire, and team with others, locally and globally.

CONNECT OUTCOMES	BY GRADE LEVEL Girls...	SAMPLE INDICATORS/SIGNS When the outcome is achieved, girls might... *
Girls develop healthy relationships: Girls learn to form and maintain meaningful and caring relationships, communicate effectively, protect their rights in relationships, and know when to seek help from others.	begin to understand how their behavior contributes to maintaining healthy relationships.	identify healthy/unhealthy behaviors (e.g., honesty, caring, bullying) when presented with a relationship scenario.
	are better able to show empathy toward others.	make empathetic statements (e.g., "I helped Kim with that because she was getting frustrated") and/or report being more caring in their interactions with others.
Girls promote cooperation and team building: Girls recognize the value of working together and learn to make decisions that benefit the whole group. They can build effective teams, learn to be accountable for their shared goals, and show recognition for others' accomplishments and contributions.	gain a better understanding of cooperative and team-building skills.	be able to identify strengths or talents that each girl brings to group projects (e.g., "Monica is good at drawing and I am a really good singer"). describe ways to make group projects more fun (e.g., switching roles, brainstorming, listening to each other).
Girls can resolve conflicts: Girls learn to recognize and analyze different conflict situations and develop skills for constructive conflict resolution and prevention.	are better able to apply basic strategies for conflict resolution when conflicts arise.	name helpful ways to deal with anger/frustration in a conflict (e.g., talk things out instead of acting out or hitting).
Girls advance diversity in a multicultural world: Girls learn to think and act in a way that promotes an inclusive environment, respecting and valuing diverse backgrounds, viewpoints, and life experiences.	begin to understand the meaning of diversity.	explore their differences and similarities (e.g., based on culture, ethnicity, ability, life experiences).
	strengthen their appreciation of differences in others.	not make fun—and might encourage others not to make fun—of those who look/talk/behave differently from themselves.
Girls feel connected to their communities, locally and globally: Girls feel that they are part of a larger community and recognize the importance of building diverse, supportive social networks for their personal and leadership development.	have greater interest in participating in community events, activities, and social networks.	positively describe their participation in at least one community event and/or activity (e.g., help at a cancer walk, start a "Park Keeper" club).
	recognize the importance of being part of a larger community.	give examples of how group/community members help and support each other (e.g., in their neighborhood, school).

*Can you think of other sample indicators/signs?

Girl Scout Brownies act to make the world a better place.

TAKE ACTION OUTCOMES	BY GRADE LEVEL Girls...	SAMPLE INDICATORS/SIGNS When the outcome is achieved, girls might... *
Girls can identify community needs: Girls learn to identify issues in their local and global communities and come up with realistic possibilities for action.	develop basic strategies to identify community issues.	use various ways to gain information about their communities (e.g., the Internet, library, personal interviews). list things about their community that are valuable and things that could be improved.
	gain a greater understanding of how Take Action Projects might impact their communities.	explain how the issue they agreed to take action on can benefit their community (e.g., other girls, families, a church).
Girls are resourceful problem solvers: Girls can use their knowledge and skills to set up and implement creative and effective "action plans," locate tools and resources they need, and know when, where, and how to enlist help from others.	are better able to develop a basic plan to reach a goal or a solution to a problem.	identify two or three steps and resources (people, materials, information) needed to reach a goal or solve a problem (e.g., how to get ready for camp).
	are better able to create alternative solutions to problems.	reflect on a real-life problem or a scenario and state an alternative solution, such as "Next time, I will do this instead."
Girls advocate for themselves and others, locally and globally: Girls develop the ability to speak out on their own behalf and seek opportunities to act and speak on behalf of others.	gain a better understanding of their rights and those of others.	name rights people have in their schools, families, or communities (e.g., to be safe, to be treated fairly, to be heard).
	learn and begin to apply basic advocacy skills.	define what advocacy means and give examples of advocates in their communities. use words or actions to show concern and intervene when another person is not being treated well (e.g., stand up for someone being teased).
Girls educate and inspire others to act: Girls learn to effectively explain their ideas to others and motivate them to get involved in community service and action.	are better able to explain their ideas or teach new skills to others.	demonstrate or teach a skill to other girls (e.g., how to sell cookies, how to make a puppet).
	can communicate their reasons for engaging in community service and action.	explain why they chose a community action project (e.g., meals to seniors, holiday gifts to needy children), how/why it benefited others, and what they learned from it.
Girls feel empowered to make a difference in the world: Girls feel empowered to use their leadership skills to effect change in their lives and their world, and feel their contributions are valued in the larger community.	increasingly feel they have important roles and responsibilities in their groups and/or communities.	describe ways their actions contributed to bettering something (for their families, neighborhood, environment).
	exhibit increased determination to create changes for themselves and others.	give examples when they succeeded in making positive change for themselves or others.

*Can you think of other sample indicators/signs?

Junior

grades 4–5

Girl Scout Juniors understand themselves and their values and use their knowledge and skills to explore the world.

DISCOVER OUTCOMES	BY GRADE LEVEL Girls...	SAMPLE INDICATORS/SIGNS When the outcome is achieved, girls might... *
Girls develop a strong sense of self: Girls have confidence in themselves and their abilities, feel they are able to achieve their goals, and form positive gender, social, and cultural identities.	are better able to recognize how situations, attitudes, and the behaviors of others affect their sense of self.	compare how various situations (home, school, etc.) bring out various aspects of self.
	gain a clearer sense of their individual identities in relation to, and apart, from outside influences.	report increased confidence in dealing with outside pressures that try to dictate their thoughts and behaviors (e.g., peer pressure, advertising, cultural traditions).
Girls develop positive values: Girls form their beliefs and values based on the Girl Scout Promise and Law, learn to consider ethical aspects of situations, and are committed to social justice and community service and action.	gain greater understanding of ethical decision-making in their lives.	give examples of using the Girl Scout Promise and Law in deciding to "do what's right."
	have increased commitment to engage in sustainable community service and action.	feel it's important to help people and the environment in ways that will have a long-term positive impact. exhibit increased interest in Take Action Projects on issues of fairness and social justice in their communities.
Girls gain practical life skills—girls practice healthy living:** Girls gain skills that prepare them for a positive, healthy, and independent future.	gain greater understanding of what it means to be emotionally and physically healthy.	describe how being stressed can affect physical health.
	are more aware of family, cultural, and media influences on making healthy choices.	list ways in which media promotes/inhibits healthy behavior (e.g., fast food ads).
Girls seek challenges in the world: Girls develop positive attitudes toward learning, seek opportunities for expanding their knowledge and skills, set challenging goals for themselves, and take appropriate risks.	increasingly recognize that positive risk-taking is important to personal growth and leadership.	when asked to identify attitudes important to accomplishing goals, mention risk-taking and give examples from their own lives.
	are better at exploring new skills and ideas.	report using a variety of resources to pursue topics of interest (e.g., the Internet, popular culture, art, poetry).
Girls develop critical thinking: Girls learn to examine ideas from a variety of viewpoints and further use critical thinking to explore implications of gender issues for their lives and their leadership development.	show greater skill in gathering and evaluating information.	consider various factors before deciding what to believe (e.g., how credible is the source of information, is there a hidden agenda).
	are better able to consider multiple perspectives on issues.	show increased interest in learning about different sides of issues (e.g., with other girls, in public forums).

*Can you think of other sample indicators/signs?

**Healthy Living is one example of a practical life skill. Outcomes and indicators for other practical skills will be developed over time.

Girl Scout Juniors care about, inspire, and team with others locally and globally.

CONNECT OUTCOMES	BY GRADE LEVEL Girls...	SAMPLE INDICATORS/SIGNS When the outcome is achieved, girls might... *
Girls develop healthy relationships: Girls learn to form and maintain meaningful and caring relationships, communicate effectively, protect their rights in relationships, and know when to seek help from others.	strengthen communication skills for maintaining healthy relationships.	name communication strategies that help them in their relationships (e.g., listening to the ideas of others, encouraging others instead of criticizing them).
	are more competent in addressing negative treatment by others.	identify bullying tactics and aggressive behaviors in others. name people they can turn to for help when dealing with difficulties in relationships.
Girls promote cooperation and team building: Girls recognize the value of working together and learn to make decisions that benefit the whole group. They can build effective teams, learn to be accountable for their shared goals, and show recognition for others' accomplishments and contributions.	are better able to initiate and maintain cooperation on their teams.	with minimal adult guidance, apply specific strategies for promoting cooperation (e.g., listening to all ideas, rotating tasks and roles, developing shared goals).
	increasingly recognize how cooperation contributes to a project's success.	consistently prefer solving problems in teams or as a group and explain why this can be more effective than working alone.
Girls can resolve conflicts: Girls learn to recognize and analyze different conflict situations and develop skills for constructive conflict resolution and prevention.	are better able to select conflict-resolution strategies to fit the situation.	describe and/or demonstrate conflict-resolution responses for various settings, such as home, school, or neighborhood. explain why one strategy works in one situation but not another (e.g., at home can resolve conflict with sibling by talking with parent; but this would not work at the playground).
	are better at analyzing conflict situations.	give reasons why they fight with each other.
Girls advance diversity in a multicultural world: Girls learn to think and act in a way that promotes an inclusive environment, respecting and valuing diverse backgrounds, viewpoints, and life experiences.	recognize the value of promoting diversity in the world.	report that it's important to promote inclusiveness in various contexts and can explain why. demonstrate increased interest in interacting with others from different backgrounds (e.g., ethnicity, culture, class, religion, gender, ability).
	develop greater awareness of various forms of discrimination in the world.	when presented with various situations (e.g., from stories, news, movies, music, or their community), identify discrimination.
Girls feel connected to their communities, locally and globally: Girls feel that they are part of a larger community and recognize the importance of building diverse, supportive social networks for their personal and leadership development.	are better able to recognize the importance of knowing about and actively participating in community groups.	identify various sources of information for what is going on in their communities (e.g., the Internet, magazines, interviews with people). describe how being involved in their communities resulted in stronger connections to others (e.g., Take Action Project resulted in an adult from the community volunteering to teach girls a particular skill).
	begin to feel part of a larger community of girls/women.	enjoy connecting with girls/women locally, nationally, or globally (e.g., through reading about them, face-to-face interactions, e-mail).

*Can you think of other sample indicators/signs?

Girl Scout Juniors act to make the world a better place.

TAKE ACTION OUTCOMES	BY GRADE LEVEL Girls...	SAMPLE INDICATORS/SIGNS When the outcome is achieved, girls might... *
Girls can identify community needs: Girls learn to identify issues in their local and global communities and come up with realistic possibilities for action.	learn to use strategies to determine issues that deserve action.	use community asset mapping to identify opportunities to better their communities.
	are better able to determine whether projects can be realistically accomplished.	consider time and/or financial constraints before selecting an issue to tackle.
Girls are resourceful problem solvers: Girls can use their knowledge and skills to set up and implement creative and effective "action plans," locate tools and resources they need, and know when, where, and how to enlist help from others.	are better able to create an "action plan" for their projects.	outline steps, resources, and time lines and assign responsibilities for their project with minimal adult guidance. report increased confidence in creating action plans for their goals.
	gain a greater ability to locate and use resources that will help accomplish their project goals.	feel confident contacting community partners who can help them achieve their goals (e.g., school officials who can display girls' fliers on bulletin boards).
Girls advocate for themselves and others, locally and globally: Girls develop the ability to speak out on their own behalf and seek opportunities to act and speak on behalf of others.	strengthen their abilities to effectively speak out or act for themselves and others.	identify concrete steps they can take to effect desired changes (e.g., whom to contact about creating safer streets for bicycling in their neighborhood).
Girls educate and inspire others to act: Girls learn to effectively explain their ideas to others and motivate them to get involved in community service and action.	learn various strategies to communicate and share Take Action Projects with others.	use various ways to tell others about their Take Action Projects (e.g., fliers, presentations). explain what makes a successful persuasive message/action for various audiences (e.g., presentation to peers, petitions to officials).
Girls feel empowered to make a difference in the world: Girls feel empowered to use their leadership skills to effect change in their lives and their world, and feel their contributions are valued in the larger community.	are more confident in their power to effect positive change.	describe various expressions of power around them (e.g., power over others, power to do something, power with others). explain how shared power helped them create better or longer-lasting changes (e.g., working together vs. doing it alone).
	feel they have greater opportunities for involvement in the decision-making of their communities.	give examples of when they participated in the decision-making processes in their Girl Scout council, church, school, etc.

*Can you think of other sample indicators/signs?

Cadette

grades 6–8

Girl Scout Cadettes understand themselves and their values and use their knowledge and skills to explore the world.

DISCOVER OUTCOMES	BY GRADE LEVEL Girls...	SAMPLE INDICATORS/SIGNS When the outcome is achieved, girls might... *
Girls develop a strong sense of self: Girls have confidence in themselves and their abilities, feel they are able to achieve their goals, and form positive gender, social, and cultural identities.	are better able to negotiate the effects of sociocultural factors, gender issues, and stereotyping/bias on their sense of self.	describe how cultural influences affect their self-image (e.g., magazines dictating "right" body shape and size; effects of racist/sexist comments). make use of strategies to resist peer pressure (e.g., communicate with confidence, take responsibility for own actions).
	show an increase in self-efficacy.	report increased belief in their ability to achieve personal goals.
Girls develop positive values: Girls form their beliefs and values based on the Girl Scout Promise and Law, learn to consider ethical aspects of situations, and are committed to social justice and community service and action.	are better able to examine their own and others' values from individual, cultural, and global perspectives.	report greater appreciation for the diversity of values based on individual and/or cultural differences.
	demonstrate increased commitment to addressing issues of fairness, ethics, and justice in their communities.	identify instances that raise questions about issues of fairness, ethics, and/or social justice in their communities.
Girls gain practical life skills—girls practice healthy living:** Girls gain skills that prepare them for a positive, healthy, and independent future.	are increasingly committed to practicing and promoting healthy behavior.	report increased interest in learning more about how exercise, diet, relaxation, and other activities can give balance to their lives.
	are more knowledgeable about how family and cultural differences affect healthy living.	give examples of various cultures' definitions and practices of healthy living.
Girls seek challenges in the world: Girls develop positive attitudes toward learning, seek opportunities for expanding their knowledge and skills, set challenging goals for themselves, and take appropriate risks.	are better able to distinguish positive and negative risk-taking.	when given risk-taking scenarios, identify and distinguish between positive and negative risk (e.g., riding with a driver who has been drinking vs. calling home for a ride even though parents will be angry).
	recognize the importance of challenging oneself for one's positive growth.	report how setting challenging goals helped them do better in school.
Girls develop critical thinking: Girls learn to examine ideas from a variety of viewpoints and further use critical thinking to explore implications of gender issues for their lives and their leadership development.	are better able to examine issues and ideas from various perspectives.	debate or discuss various perspectives on an issue they are concerned about (e.g., women's rights, global warming).
	have increased understanding of positive and negative ways that media impact their own and others' lives.	give examples of how TV shows can promote sexism, racism, and other -isms or how the Internet can promote freedom of information or allow disinformation.

*Can you think of other sample indicators/signs?

**Healthy Living is one example of a practical life skill. Outcomes and indicators for other practical skills will be developed over time.

Girl Scout Cadettes care about, inspire, and team with others locally and globally.

CONNECT OUTCOMES	BY GRADE LEVEL Girls...	SAMPLE INDICATORS/SIGNS When the outcome is achieved, girls might... *
Girls develop healthy relationships: Girls learn to form and maintain meaningful and caring relationships, communicate effectively, protect their rights in relationships, and know when to seek help from others.	have more positive, trusting relationships with others.	report having at least one girl or adult they can talk to about anything.
	are able to use positive communication and relationship-building skills.	give examples of behaviors they use to promote mutual respect, trust, and understanding.
	feel more comfortable with new feelings that accompany adolescence and ways of expressing feelings in relationships, including sexual feelings.	talk about healthy decision-making (e.g., encouraging self-respect in themselves and others) when presented with relationship scenarios.
Girls promote cooperation and team building: Girls recognize the value of working together and learn to make decisions that benefit the whole group. They can build effective teams, learn to be accountable for their shared goals, and show recognition for others' accomplishments and contributions.	have a greater understanding of team building.	list criteria for what makes a good team (e.g., clear roles, trust, respect, diversity).
	are better able to address obstacles to effective group work and team building.	describe obstacles to group work (e.g., not being willing to compromise, concern with individual interests over group goals, always wanting to be the person talking) and suggest possible solutions.
Girls can resolve conflicts: Girls learn to recognize and analyze different conflict situations and develop skills for constructive conflict resolution and prevention.	strengthen their conflict resolution and prevention strategies.	say how they manage their emotions (e.g., anger, hurt) to diffuse a conflict situation (e.g., don't lose their temper).
	have a greater understanding of how conflict-resolution skills contribute to effective leadership.	give examples of how their conflict-resolution skills helped them succeed on a project.
Girls advance diversity in a multicultural world: Girls learn to think and act in a way that promotes an inclusive environment, respecting and valuing diverse backgrounds, viewpoints, and life experiences.	are more aware of the issues, perspectives, and experiences of people from various backgrounds, locally and globally.	identify main challenges and privileges that various groups experience in today's world (e.g., women and men, ethnicities, abilities).
	learn strategies for promoting diversity and creating more inclusive environments.	actively include people of diverse backgrounds in their activities/events. actively encourage others to behave in inclusive ways (e.g., petition for a wheelchair-accessible park gazebo, use effective ways to speak out against exclusion and discrimination).
	can examine the negative impact of stereotyping, prejudice, discrimination, and privilege on their lives and the lives of others.	when given examples from the media, describe the negative impact of stereotyping and prejudice (based on ethnicity, religion, language, class, sexuality, gender, and ability).
Girls feel connected to their communities, locally and globally: Girls feel that they are part of a larger community and recognize the importance of building diverse, supportive social networks for their personal and leadership development.	strengthen existing relationships and seek to create new connections with others in their communities.	use various ways to connect with others, locally and globally (e.g., the Internet, get-togethers, *destinations*, events). feel more confident contacting community members for help with community service and action projects (e.g., teachers, youth organizations, after-school clubs).
	gain greater understanding of the importance of community networks for themselves and others.	describe how their participation in larger communities supported their personal and leadership goals (e.g., provided safe environment, helped gain skills).

*Can you think of other sample indicators/signs?

Girl Scout Cadettes act to make the world a better place.

TAKE ACTION OUTCOMES	BY GRADE LEVEL Girls...	SAMPLE INDICATORS/SIGNS When the outcome is achieved, girls might... *
Girls can identify community needs: Girls learn to identify issues in their local and global communities and come up with realistic possibilities for action.	strengthen their ability to decide which community issue deserves action.	report using a variety of tools (e.g., community mapping, interviewing, observations) to identify needs, assets, and potential impact of their planned projects.
	begin to address deeper causes of issues in their communities.	identify multiple causes for a problem they wish to address. explain the difference between a quick fix and long-term solutions (e.g., reading to someone learning English as a second language vs. teaching someone to read).
Girls are resourceful problem solvers: Girls can use their knowledge and skills to set up and implement creative and effective "action plans," locate tools and resources they need, and know when, where, and how to enlist help from others.	are able to create and implement detailed action plans for their projects.	demonstrate independence in thinking through the required components of their action plans (e.g., location of resources, time lines, responsibilities). report being more able to keep themselves "on track," requesting adult help if needed.
	increasingly seek out community support and resources to help achieve their goals.	identify people/organizations in their communities to help on some aspect of their project (e.g., obtain editing guidance for media projects).
Girls advocate for themselves and others, locally and globally: Girls develop the ability to speak out on their own behalf and seek opportunities to act and speak on behalf of others.	recognize the importance of advocacy in accomplishing positive changes for themselves and others.	give examples of how youth can influence and/or participate in community decision-making (e.g., influence the library to remain open longer, start a teen hotline, form an antidiscrimination group).
	gain greater ability to use specific advocacy skills to address issues of interest.	report using various strategies to speak out for themselves and others on issues of interest (e.g., writing letters, petitions, creating public announcements).
Girls educate and inspire others to act: Girls learn to effectively explain their ideas to others and motivate them to get involved in community service and action.	show increased commitment to educate others on how to better their communities.	organize a show-and-tell for younger Girl Scouts to educate them about how to be more active in community affairs.
	are better able to identify and select various methods for informing others about their Take Action Projects.	report knowing how to tailor their messages to various audiences (e.g., young girls vs. senior citizens).
Girls feel empowered to make a difference in the world: Girls feel empowered to use their leadership skills to effect change in their lives and their world, and feel their contributions are valued in the larger community.	feel more valued by others for their ability to apply leaderships skills toward positive change.	feel that their opinions, ideas, and contributions are taken seriously by adults. express pride that their Take Action Projects improved functioning of some aspect of their communities (e.g., contributed to cleaner air, safer streets, better opportunities for young people).
	have increased confidence to participate in decision-making processes in their groups or communities.	show interest in providing and/or receiving input from community members on community issues.

*Can you think of other sample indicators/signs?

GIRL SCOUT GRADE LEVEL

Senior

grades 9–10

Girl Scout Seniors understand themselves and their values and use their knowledge and skills to explore the world.

DISCOVER OUTCOMES	BY GRADE LEVEL Girls...	SAMPLE INDICATORS/SIGNS When the outcome is achieved, girls might... *
Girls develop a strong sense of self: Girls have confidence in themselves and their abilities, feel they are able to achieve their goals, and form positive gender, social, and cultural identities.	are better able to recognize and address personal and social barriers to reaching personal goals.	make connections between societal issues (e.g., prejudice based on gender or race) and their opportunities to achieve goals. report on ways they overcame gender, ethnic, and/or economic challenges to achieving their goals.
	are better able to recognize the multiple demands and expectations of others while establishing their own individuality.	describe challenges they face in finding a balance between accepting group beliefs and thinking/making decisions for themselves.
Girls develop positive values: Girls form their beliefs and values based on the Girl Scout Promise and Law, learn to consider ethical aspects of situations, and are committed to social justice and community service and action.	are better able to recognize and resolve ethical dilemmas.	give examples of making ethical decisions in their everyday lives and can explain why they made them (e.g., consider both direct and indirect consequences of their actions).
	strengthen their own and others' commitment to being socially, politically, and environmentally engaged citizens of their communities.	report increased positive attitudes of social responsibility and citizenship.
Girls gain practical life skills—girls practice healthy living:** Girls gain skills that prepare them for a positive, healthy, and independent future.	act as role models for younger girls in making healthy choices.	describe strategies for resisting pressure to engage in unhealthy behaviors (e.g., alcohol use or unhealthy dieting).
	show cultural sensitivity in their efforts to promote healthy living in their communities.	report increased knowledge of specific health needs in their diverse communities (e.g., responsive to religious or cultural beliefs).
Girls seek challenges in the world: Girls develop positive attitudes toward learning, seek opportunities for expanding their knowledge and skills, set challenging goals for themselves, and take appropriate risks.	demonstrate increased enthusiasm for learning new skills and ideas and expanding existing ones.	increasingly offer their own ideas for exploring new topics or making existing ones more challenging.
	show increased courage to challenge their own and others' beliefs and opinions.	engage in a discussion with someone who has different political views. express preferences even when they differ from the majority's opinion.
Girls develop critical thinking: Girls learn to examine ideas from a variety of viewpoints and further use critical thinking to explore implications of gender issues for their lives and their leadership development.	are better able to analyze their own and others' thinking processes.	give examples of the steps they followed and why they made a specific decision or formed an opinion.
	apply critical thinking skills to challenge stereotypes and biases in their lives and in society.	question assumptions behind inequities they encounter (e.g., female athletes earning less than male athletes).

*Can you think of other sample indicators/signs?

**Healthy Living is one example of a practical life skill. Outcomes and indicators for other practical skills will be developed over time.

Girl Scout Seniors care about, inspire, and team with others, locally and globally.

CONNECT OUTCOMES	BY GRADE LEVEL Girls...	SAMPLE INDICATORS/SIGNS When the outcome is achieved, girls might... *
Girls develop healthy relationships: Girls learn to form and maintain meaningful and caring relationships, communicate effectively, protect their rights in relationships, and know when to seek help from others.	are better able to recognize and address challenges to forming and maintaining healthy relationships with others.	recognize that people hold different beliefs about relationships (e.g., based on gender, culture). identify behaviors that hinder the development of positive relationships (e.g., backstabbing, gossip).
	have increased knowledge of what healthy dating entails.	report that it is important to be able to communicate their needs effectively. recognize unhealthy dating behaviors when presented with a dating scenario.
Girls promote cooperation and team building: Girls recognize the value of working together and learn to make decisions that benefit the whole group. They can build effective teams, learn to be accountable for their shared goals, and show recognition for others' accomplishments and contributions.	strengthen their abilities to build effective teams to accomplish shared goals.	identify specific strategies for building effective teams (e.g., paying attention to interests, strengths, team dynamics). demonstrate that they can reach consensus on common goals.
	are committed to mentoring others on effective strategies for cooperative work and team building.	help others work better as a team (e.g., encourage them to reach consensus on project goals, create "listening" exercises for other girls, recognize each others' achievements).
Girls can resolve conflicts: Girls learn to recognize and analyze different conflict situations and develop skills for constructive conflict resolution and prevention.	can increasingly apply effective strategies for conflict resolution and prevention.	report using effective anger-management skills and strategies.
	are better able to analyze conflict situations in their communities and globally, and offer possible solutions.	identify deeper social roots of conflicts among various groups in their communities (e.g., conflicting interests, racism, sexism, other forms of prejudice). describe how certain conflicts in their communities can be avoided by applying prevention strategies they learned.
Girls advance diversity in a multicultural world: Girls learn to think and act in a way that promotes an inclusive environment, respecting and valuing diverse backgrounds, viewpoints, and life experiences.	are actively engaged in promoting diversity and tolerance.	create materials to educate others on how to contribute to more inclusive environments with their peers, in school, in their neighborhoods. (e.g., Web sites, how-to guides, events).
	are increasingly able to address challenges to promoting inclusive attitudes and diversity.	plan activities/events showing the harmful consequences of prejudice and discrimination on people in their communities. place high value on empathy and open-mindedness when interacting with people from diverse backgrounds.
Girls feel connected to their communities, locally and globally: Girls feel that they are part of a larger community and recognize the importance of building diverse, supportive social networks for their personal and leadership development.	actively seek to bring people together in local and global networks.	give an example of organizing a local or global event that brought together diverse members of their communities. develop friendships with Girl Guides from other countries (e.g., e-mail pals, joint international projects, visits to World Centers).
	feel that their connections with diverse members of their communities are important resources for personal and leadership development.	make friends with girls/women through the World Association of Girl Guides and Girl Scouts (WAGGGS) and can explain why these connections are important to them.

*Can you think of other sample indicators/signs?

Girl Scout Seniors act to make the world a better place.

TAKE ACTION OUTCOMES	BY GRADE LEVEL Girls...	SAMPLE INDICATORS/SIGNS When the outcome is achieved, girls might... *
Girls can identify community needs: Girls learn to identify issues in their local and global communities and come up with realistic possibilities for action.	are more skilled in identifying their local or global communities' needs that they can realistically address.	report considering multiple factors before deciding on the appropriateness of a project for their community (e.g., feasibility, balance of assets and needs, sustainable impact). seek advice from community members/leaders before selecting issues for action.
	choose Take Action Projects that aim to address deeper causes of issues in their communities.	feel confident using tools that help them identify root causes of community problems (e.g., causal mapping).
Girls are resourceful problem solvers: Girls can use their knowledge and skills to set up and implement creative and effective "action plans," locate tools and resources they need, and know when, where, and how to enlist help from others.	are better able to effectively plan and carry out action projects with minimal adult guidance.	create detailed action plans, organize, and coordinate with others in the community, managing time and anticipating possible problems and resource needs on their own.
	are able to assess their progress and adjust strategies as necessary.	identify alternative ways to accomplish goals if initial plans prove unsuccessful. identify things they could do better and/or differently next time they work on a community service or action project.
Girls advocate for themselves and others, locally and globally: Girls develop the ability to speak out on their own behalf and seek opportunities to act and speak on behalf of others.	have a greater understanding of how the decisions and policies of various institutions have effects on their lives and the lives of others.	report increased knowledge about how public decisions in their schools, communities, and local governments affect people's private lives (e.g., decisions about education, juvenile justice).
	use advocacy skills and knowledge to be more active on behalf of a cause, issue or person, locally or globally.	give examples of advocating for an issue in their school or neighborhood (e.g., more healthful cafeteria food, increased awareness of eating disorders, reproductive health, effects of poverty).
Girls educate and inspire others to act: Girls learn to effectively explain their ideas to others and motivate them to get involved in community service and action.	are better at inspiring and mobilizing others to become more engaged in community service and action.	shape messages (e.g., in a flier, speech, publication, or Web campaign) to explain the importance of taking action on an issue they care about. organize an awareness day in their schools on an issue they care about (e.g., emotional health, Internet safety).
Girls feel empowered to make a difference in the world: Girls feel empowered to use their leadership skills to effect change in their lives and their world, and feel their contributions are valued in the larger community.	are better able to address challenges to their feeling of empowerment.	identify internal and/or external barriers to feeling empowered to create change (e.g., not being taken seriously because they are "just kids"). describe strategies for ensuring that their voices and opinions are heard.
	feel that they have greater access to community resources and more equal relationships with adults in their communities.	report that adults in their communities invite their input and/or participation in community affairs.

*Can you think of other sample indicators/signs?

Girl Scout Ambassadors understand themselves and their values and use their knowledge and skills to explore the world.

DISCOVER OUTCOMES	BY GRADE LEVEL Girls...	SAMPLE INDICATORS/SIGNS When the outcome is achieved, girls might... *
Girls develop a strong sense of self: Girls have confidence in themselves and their abilities, feel they are able to achieve their goals, and form positive gender, social, and cultural identities.	feel they are better equipped to pursue future/life goals.	report that they have options and possibilities for pursuing life/career goals. report increased confidence to get the job/education they envision.
	increase their sense of autonomy.	report being more self-reliant.
Girls develop positive values: Girls form their beliefs and values based on the Girl Scout Promise and Law, learn to consider ethical aspects of situations, and are committed to social justice and community service and action.	act consistently with a considered and self-determined set of values.	choose educational and career goals in line with the values they consider important.
	demonstrate commitment to promoting sustainable solutions to regional, national, and/or global problems.	report increased interest in learning more about making a sustainable impact beyond their local communities.
Girls gain practical life skills—girls practice healthy living:** Girls gain skills that prepare them for a positive, healthy, and independent future.	are better able to identify health issues in their lives, their local communities, and globally.	report using self-care practices to bring balance to their lives. identify ways their school's health education could better address the needs of young women.
	are more interested in leading and/or participating in advocacy projects related to health issues, globally or locally.	report increased knowledge of organizations that advocate for health-related issues, locally or globally.
Girls seek challenges in the world: Girls develop positive attitudes toward learning, seek opportunities for expanding their knowledge and skills, set challenging goals for themselves, and take appropriate risks.	increasingly set challenging goals for the future.	see themselves in roles/positions they previously considered unattainable.
	have increased confidence to discuss and address challenging issues and contradictions in their lives and in their local and global communities.	look for ways personal habits conflict with achieving goals that are important to them (e.g., fighting global warming). learn more about a controversial issue from someone who has experienced injustice or from a victim's advocate.
Girls develop critical thinking: Girls learn to examine ideas from a variety of viewpoints and further use critical thinking to explore implications of gender issues for their lives and their leadership development.	are increasingly able to address local/global/societal barriers to women's leadership.	discuss various obstacles facing women leaders now and in the past (e.g., discrimination based on gender, race, class, ability, etc.). express interest in Take Action Projects that address gender inequality locally or globally.

*Can you think of other sample indicators/signs?

**Healthy Living is one example of a practical life skill. Outcomes and indicators for other practical skills will be developed over time.

Girl Scout Ambassadors care about, inspire, and team with others locally and globally.

CONNECT OUTCOMES	BY GRADE LEVEL Girls...	SAMPLE INDICATORS/SIGNS When the outcome is achieved, girls might... *
Girls develop healthy relationships: Girls learn to form and maintain meaningful and caring relationships, communicate effectively, protect their rights in relationships, and know when to seek help from others.	strengthen strategies for maintaining healthy relationships.	give examples of using assertive behaviors and might explain when and why these work/don't work.
	are better able to protect their rights in relationships.	actively seek information on healthy dating behaviors (e.g., how to avoid risky sexual activity, where to get help for abusive relationships). report knowing whom to contact when faced with unhealthy relationships (e.g., a hotline, school counselor, trusted adults).
Girls promote cooperation and team building: Girls recognize the value of working together and learn to make decisions that benefit the whole group. They can build effective teams, learn to be accountable for their shared goals, and show recognition for others' accomplishments and contributions.	are able to promote cooperation and effective team building in their communities.	describe how their Take Action Project encouraged sustained cooperation among various people/organizations in their communities.
	recognize the value of cooperation and team building for effective leadership and for their future careers.	report that cooperation and teambuilding skills helped them in other spheres of their lives.
Girls can resolve conflicts: Girls learn to recognize and analyze different conflict situations and develop skills for constructive conflict resolution and prevention.	are better able to develop their own approaches to conflict resolution and prevention in their lives and communities.	give examples of how they adapted conflict-resolution strategies to personal situations (e.g., argument with parent or at a teen dance).
	increasingly apply conflict-resolution skills to working toward peaceful and fair relations in their communities.	report using conflict-resolution skills to contribute to peace and fairness in their communities (e.g., become peer mediators at school).
Girls advance diversity in a multicultural world: Girls learn to think and act in a way that promotes an inclusive environment, respecting and valuing diverse backgrounds, viewpoints, and life experiences.	are actively engaged in promoting diversity and tolerance, locally and/or globally.	give examples of meaningful collaboration with people from diverse backgrounds for their global Take Action Projects.
	are increasingly able to address challenges to promoting inclusive attitudes and diversity locally and/or globally.	identify the main reasons that prevent people from embracing diversity (e.g., racism, sexism, lack of education, lack of empathy) and can suggest possible solutions (e.g., increase understanding by educating people about diverse cultural values and traditions).
Girls feel connected to their communities, locally and globally: Girls feel that they are part of a larger community and recognize the importance of building diverse, supportive social networks for their personal and leadership development.	have extensive feelings of connection with their local and global communities.	report more positive attitudes toward different members of their communities. place high value on providing support for diverse members of their communities.

*Can you think of other sample indicators/signs?

Girl Scout Ambassadors act to make the world a better place.

TAKE ACTION OUTCOMES	BY GRADE LEVEL Girls...	SAMPLE INDICATORS/SIGNS When the outcome is achieved, girls might... *
Girls can identify community needs: Girls learn to identify issues in their local and global communities and come up with realistic possibilities for action.	are more skilled in identifying issues that balance feasibility with achieving long-term changes in their local or global communities.	identify community partners that can continue their project goals into the future.
	choose Take Action Projects that aim to address deeper causes of issues in their communities.	interview staff and residents of a homeless shelter to identify root cause of homelessness in the community.
Girls are resourceful problem solvers: Girls can use their knowledge and skills to set up and implement creative and effective "action plans," locate tools and resources they need, and know when, where, and how to enlist help from others.	are better able to independently plan, organize, and manage Take Action Projects.	report increased knowledge and skill in various aspects of project planning and implementation. monitor their own progress and determine criteria for success.
	actively seek partnerships to achieve greater community participation and impact for their Take Action Projects.	describe their efforts to engage community partners—locally or globally—in the implementation of community service and action projects. explain how partnerships with others maximize the impact of their Take Action Projects.
Girls advocate for themselves and others, locally and globally: Girls develop the ability to speak out on their own behalf and seek opportunities to act and speak on behalf of others.	recognize that they have the rights and abilities to participate in the development of public policy that affects their lives and the lives of others.	report increased interest and confidence in participating in projects or initiatives that promote positive social changes.
	are better able to consider the community/global impact of their advocacy efforts.	describe how their advocacy efforts helped their community or the broader society.
	actively seek partnerships with other organizations that provide support and resources for their advocacy efforts.	report working with organizations that share their advocacy goals.
Girls educate and inspire others to act: Girls learn to effectively explain their ideas to others and motivate them to get involved in community service and action.	are better able to evaluate the effectiveness of their efforts to reach/educate diverse audiences and can adjust their communication strategies accordingly.	implement innovative ways to access hard-to-reach audiences (e.g., using the Internet to engage remote rural populations). work with other youth/community organizations to spread their messages more effectively.
Girls feel empowered to make a difference in the world: Girls feel empowered to use their leadership skills to effect change in their lives and their world, and feel their contributions are valued in the larger community.	feel capable of using their skills to better the functioning and governance of communities, locally or globally.	create an action plan that could be implemented to include more young people in setting town priorities.
	feel their projects and ideas are valued/respected by stakeholders in their local and/or global communities.	give examples of positive reports (e.g., local news coverage) about their Take Action Projects.

*Can you think of other sample indicators/signs?

Acknowledgments

The information in this document draws upon an extensive review of available research and professional literature in the fields of education, youth development, psychology, and related disciplines. To obtain a bibliography, write to gsresearch@girlscouts.org.

The New Girl Scout Leadership Experience was made possible thanks to the contributions of girls and adults throughout the Girl Scout community and experts from a variety of fields. Girl Scouts of the USA thanks:

Girls in and out of Girl Scouts, volunteers, and Girl Scout council staff from Arizona, California, Connecticut, Colorado, the District of Columbia, Florida, Georgia, Indiana, Maryland, Massachusetts, Michigan, Missouri, New Jersey, New York, North Carolina, Ohio, Texas, Utah, and Washington that took part in focus groups and council and regional work sessions

195 Girl Scout councils that participated in conference calls

4,500 Girl Scouts and volunteers who took part in strategy cafés (informal discussion forums) during the 2005 National Council Session

Members of the Program Advisory Group Councils:
Girl Scout Council of the Congaree Area, Inc.; Girl Scouts of Freedom Valley; Girl Scouts of Kentuckiana, Inc., Girl Scouts of Manitou Council, Inc.; Girl Scouts of Maumee Valley Council, Inc.; Girl Scouts of Southwest Texas; Girl Scouts of Santa Clara County

Members of the Program Gap Team:
Girl Scouts of Central Maryland, Inc.; Glowing Embers Girl Scout Council, Inc.; Girl Scout Great Rivers Council, Inc.; Girl Scouts of Pine Valley Council, Inc.

Experts in the youth development field from Connecticut College, Harvard Family Research Project/Harvard Graduate School of Education, Innovation Center for Community and Youth Development, National 4-H, the Search Institute, University of Arizona, University of Illinois, University of Minnesota, The Forum for Youth Investment, and University of Michigan

ActKnowledge, a research organization dedicated to working with not-for-profits, foundations, and governmental agencies that uses the Theory of Change process as a participatory tool to help organizations create detailed plans for decision-making and evaluation

SPEC Associates, a research and evaluation firm and a long-time consultant to Girl Scouts of the USA in its efforts to measure program processes and outcomes

Smarty Pants, a youth market research and strategic consulting organization

Goodwin Group, a corporate design firm specializing in the youth industry